Your Ten Favorite Words

Also by Reb Livingston:

Pterodactyls Soar Again (Whole Coconut Chapbook Series)

Wanton Textiles (co-author, No Tell Books)

The Bedside Guide to No Tell Motel (co-editor with Molly Arden, No Tell Books)

The Bedside Guide to No Tell Motel - Second Floor (co-editor with Molly Arden, No Tell Books)

Your Ten Favorite Words

by

Reb Livingston

Coconut Books

Atlanta, GA

2007

Copyright © 2007 by Reb Livingston

Published by Coconut Books

www.coconutpoetry.org

All rights reserved

ISBN: 978-0-6151-6182-2

Cover Design: Meghan Punschke

Proofreader: Joseph Massey

Contents

Our Rascal Asses

Pine Box   9
No-Tell   10
No Bra Required   11
Almost Took a Lover Once   12
My Lover Beside   13
Things Get   14
Tonight I Doze   15
They Say He Was a Very Great Man   16
He Will   17
Seven Spell   18
Inept Photography   20
What Doesn't Do   22
Good Night, I Swear   23
My Uncommon Concubine   24
God Gets Close   26
I Am in Love and You Are Not 27

Unsweet and Looking for a Fix

At Last and Everlasting 33
Clutch 36
The Miser(ables)   37
The Love Story 38
Nothing Like Us   40
Quantity of the Quality   41
Still Feeling It 42
Poem for Make-Believe 43

Brunch with Cordelia   44
Requiem   45
Off Vermont   46
Wifely Attempt at Poem   48
No Room at the Necropolis   50
What There Wasn't Time to Mention   51
Rare Hawk Evident   55

Burgers and Pitchforks

The Spirit to Adopt   59
On Realizing There Won't Be a Ceremony   60
Finite and Fortnight   61
Ours Alone   62
Kinda, Yeah   63
Who the Man Was   64
Luna Park   65
Wanting to Be a Man of Saturn   66
My Lover Never   67
Retention   69
Brevity is Not My Soul   70
Apologies for Ice   71
Cold Storage   73
Much We Could Do   74
Whatnot Tribute   75

Acknowledgements   77

Our Rascal Asses

The Smitten Girl [to The Man with the Pretty Chin]: Will you be using your charm for good or injury?

The Heart Specter [murmuring]: (C)harm for G(o)od!

Pine Box

Maybe I'm impressed by church light.
Split pews didn't part the Red Sea –
neither did diagonal stripes or rubbing shoulders.

When I say *impressed* I'm not talking
penis, so put it back in your pocket,
those slithering slacks that make me

wonder if you've started working out.
This is about art, being over it and being good.
That's what I came for. I'm so over it.

See God. See Moon. See Conifer. Over.

But all this stained glass, the bright shades
pined against night – Sure.

Come hither. The man in the tower
just stepped out for juice and right
now I sense a potent sparkle from your beacon.

I'm talking literal,
I truly believe you're a ship
full of tiny wisps waving shiny lighters
screaming *Encore!*

Cruise liner, tug boat, sinking barge of coal,
what do I know?
Hurry, before I require downfall.
Careful, those rocks are sharp!

No-Tell

Not as unlikely as I'll attest,
nor as disagreeable as assessed.

Why else do motel maids
trouble knocking? God bless

America, for begetting
a place where we could meet

and do this.

No Bra Required

Someone scrawled
funny words
on our underwear.

Our underwear,
way too loose

on our rascal asses.
*We must realize ourselves
into those big britches,*

you declare. Love
in a handbasket. Hell
in my heart. My camisole,

yours, evermore. Never
have I believed in polygamy
more than I do rising this

daybreak.

Almost Took a Lover Once

He was dark brilliance and moans
(his moans, girlish and dusk, yet I gushed)
He tried to take me to his room
(for he had succeeded, others, redundant)

He tried to get into mine
(he was pleasing, so pleasing, he fissured my mind)
He warned he would snore
(I insisted he keep his shirt on, he was shade,

he agreed). His black hairs snagged the fibers of my gown
(if I was murdered, he would have been the only suspect)
Daylight came, my freckles began to dawn
For like I said, he was dark and brilliant and when

He turned spectral, forgot quick enough

My Lover Beside

O how he positions his palms
presses his thumb

above, almost historical
mouths the shoulder

clenched as crossword
puzzles, scribbled and clasped

He asks about quality,
its fuzzy whisper a hidden, hungry

thing
He gasps *Something queer is going on*

I nearly faint

Things Get

To wax the instant – things get rhapsodic, slash – deepen – enigma – things get trusty, so little to celebrate – the topics pervasive – things get inarticulate – and I never dreamed I'd get buttressed by you, my status quo goes throes, tell me more about the perspective of that female character, my ulysses goes soft – things get close – drags me east, let's ward off voices – tabulated – destabilized – gleefullized – spurned and provoked. How *om* became counterculture in the first place – I do not know.

Tonight I Doze

Because insomnia is no fun and who's dark and frilly now?
Not me, yes me, oh woe whoa, what did we step in this time?

Everything was textbook sweetness, tv show thrillingness
and then, then, fuck you and your then, hairy hands

spiral eyeballs, pat and rub, whimsy stick, I saw you
peek-a-wink, yes you simply offered alternatives.

I lapped lipped your radiation, let you sneak in the side
kissed cursed your crooked eyelids, lived loved your false greetings.

Those were good days, those three, they shouldn't have ended but
clocks, they were born to run, hah, I'm trying to be funny.

You made me nervous, bulbous, fortuitous, I'm using big words
and I don't know what they mean. I squealed for ya.

That's what I did and you got sleepy and said now we could sleep.
I didn't want to sleep, I wanted to talk and go back in time

so there'd be nothing to talk about and start over and graze
past, shake hands, shake an ankle, kiss kiss. There was that

stairwell, that lost opportunity of steps and railings.
Now I'm fat, draped in flannel and you take too damn long

to respond and never answer important questions
like . . .

They Say He Was a Very Great Man

Ruled, loved and received
describe my reign
in order of importance.

I must twist and dodge
grab your wrist
and insist, no sobs

no eye flutters
in order to be honest.
We sup hot flounder

relish your book club tales.
Mmm our thoughts melt nicely.
I rule you like an antelope.

Love you as a martyr.
I receive your licked envelope
and fumble for stamps.

He Will

He will want the vulture. He will put on a cotton button-down and tuck your kisses in his collar – ring around the rosie. Oblige the whorehound, oblige all his throbbing manparts. This is how you seduce him. This is his nice-to-meet-you hat and this is your throes-into-woe hat. This is how you lace your bra and this explains curtains and what possibly could you better do with this extraordinary walking cane, except beat down those amorous arms, make them flail faster, bound down harder. This is how you deduce him. Lean into his face when speaking, stare at his pretty chin, don't threaten the vulture perched on his shoulder, it knows the meaning of humans and hasn't eaten for months. You're not human, you're like the Marlboro Man, horse dust, salt, death sex, dust lust. He will want the vulture to stay. Oblige them. Show your pockets. This is how you reduce him. Ashes, ashes – he falls in love.

Seven Spell

conjured in a closet,
seven minutes in a delusive boon

deep breaths shallow,
ankles stretched, entwined

ribs padded with throbs,
bells and trance

it never ended and then
it ended

the spell distant,
retrospect, precious

the doorways, hall-
ways, the fleeting pitter

patters gaze
up a long flight of stairs

something's still
there to behold

is it sorcery or charm?
invoke a comely name for it

recall your palms
flattening my thrum,

my thrum, my good judgment groped,
ravaged, delirious

Inept Photography

Arch your back
clicked the camera lens
which makes sounds, but
doesn't and
that makes sense

when it's unfocused

Found your apologia under the pillow
Pulled out all the verbs
you left me
with this:

kosher   principled   elixir
         pipe   porcupine
tasteful   darling

Writing means
very little

I only sing when I'm desperate
or drunk

My song is fool and flash and a mouthful of
crooked hairy toes (if only it ended there)

The backdrop: blowing curtains and dust bunnies and
wrinkled sheets and candle-waxed headboard

The harder we kissed, the more pointless

you became
the sloppier
my chin
(shiny, kind of drooly)
your shadow, my torso

most unflattering
angle

What Doesn't Do

Trolls took my terry clots and I don't like to drive when a long poem kicks me in the shiver chambers making me hallucinate experts and loving Shiva. Am I the flesh that's lost her way? Or full of graves, wasting, washing the back of my neck in case he goes there, rather that than getting naked or installing that new furnace? Have you seen the moon tonight? Apparently it's enough, for a night.

Good Night, I Swear

There is a bruise to your breath, my love, that I swear you commanded. Yes, you're sitting very near, but this is public where there's none of that allowed and you're wearing jeans and I'm possessing knowledge of your goblin knees. That's a textbook secret I'm keeping. You have to go home now and so should I and this is sounding worse every minute and you're looking better, my love. Hellos are nimble and goodbyes are curt and you, noble soul who allows me to undress him, grader of my internal monologues, oh icon of stodgy sexiness, I submit, I too go weak in the . . . oh that good night, was that supposed to be gentle? There are aches and they're alarming and damp and unmentioned, I swear.

My Uncommon Concubine

My uncommon concubine misexplains pain for I misremember his printed face for ease and translation.

My uncommon concubine looks a wince in need of a gesture all his own.

My uncommon concubine piles haphazardly, piles nickel-plated steel, piles words in occasional lumps and gusts and he's a bit more difficult than the average concubine and I could cure him of all stiffness, if only he read my words.

My uncommon concubine is my pupil and instructor and holds my door and sends me his bills.

My uncommon concubine is not my gigolo.

I have no say over his undergarments.

I say, *You're not finished. Keep at it.*

I say, *How about another? How about you be quiet? How about you run to the store for strawberries?*

My uncommon concubine is intelligent. For a concubine.

I never discuss my love for my uncommon concubine.

I have much love for my uncommon concubine.

Question to uncommon concubine: Is it desire or disdain you hide with silence?

Statement to uncommon concubine: You are my uncommon concubine and you are intact and I could cure you of your sex-doll status with knitting needles and Christmas cotton.

Admonishment to uncommon concubine: You tend to repeat yourself; repetition is something you do often.

Conciliation to uncommon concubine: I'd promote you to full-fledged spouse.

If only it was allowed.

God Gets Close

You scratch the garnets on everything you unclasp

There's a missing set of silverware and freezer full of untouched waffles

God gets close and you depart with only trinkets in the night

You are the hand in the pocket of a ghost with a waning appetite

Tomorrow I'll drop an opal down my camisole and draw a map

I Am in Love and You Are Not

you before sunrise
you not singing "Here Comes the Sun"
me not thinking it's all right
me missing syllables
me staring at your arm
slung like it belongs

you looking for lark
you with too many
you with that Anglo-American
quality, practically one of us
but improved, with that added world
perspective that makes girls go Italian

go to the video store, go
on explaining their facial expressions
in case you're considering
their eye color
you mention jade
you squinting

your glasses, gauze and I
bleed like sunset
no, shine like moon, a shine
getting fierce
a shine dimming
the shine you see through to see

her, maybe all of them
how many more?

I'd like to know
you holding the pearl
you swallowing the clam

me so dizzy, me looking back
long time
seeing plaid
seeing it soft
seeing daybreak
flash, burn
I should be blind by now

Yes, I really should

Unsweet and Looking for a Fix

The Man with the Pretty Chin: Darling, there is no false melody. Accept your inner leprosy.

The Smitten Girl: I lament these incessant impulses. My eyes. All gray and low.

The Heart Specter: (L)amen(t), (l)amen(t), (l)amen(t).

At Last and Everlasting

This is where we surpass the love of mothmen and mothers

and foretell burnt wings, death by hummingbird

estimators arriving much too late to the scene

and this is usually when he laces her back

and then his coffee

there's hot comfort on the side, comfort belonging to someone else

and he named the island after another because the name he wanted was forbidden

and it began in a valley, ravaged by cargo trains

dragging loads of coal, dusty smutty coal

suck the coal, pray for the coal, what's wrong with you

she specifically said never kiss the coal and there you go

quarreling with bed lamps, attracting the wrong creatures

pick these walnuts, peel the rot, watch these girls

these ones aren't permitted past the church

and these can go till the end of the lane

whatever you do, don't let them rip off the wings

girls are so cruel

coal-sucking Venuses, cartwheel-thrusting harlots

and when he says coming through, he means passing through

that means you ready the casserole and let him roll

and she means it all, every bit, and knows that cornbread will make you sick

and there's tainted tuna for dessert and those late trains that

she doesn't want you talking to – sound amazing

and they're totally different in the dark

fluttering, channeling their depressing little omens

dreamy romantic trains and moths, chugging towards that light

and she's threatening to hang herself and she's asking for $50

and she has a cat and there's a lot of foreclosures in this city

and who would have thought anti-lock brakes would shake like that

and who would have thought kissing coal could be like this

there's a thousand chemical reactions and they all warm apples into decay, apples loving their creaking branches

even after dropped, watching from the ground

those apples know all

the squirrels pilfering nuts, lavish deceitful squirrels

brown licey beautiful squirrels, it's time to rethink the medication

time to give up the ghost, she doesn't see it anyhow

she's shutting the ambulance door, the girls whisper *emergency*

the girls twirl their mustaches and tie the specter to the tracks

the girls tell the specter to step into that light and leave their
    moths alone

bitchy home-wrecking wraith, dirty train-hopping banshee

it's a miracle, it's forever, we're doomed

we're wearing matching smarty pants, we're disasters, we're marooned,

festooned with soot and stickiness, we've come a long way

through all that haze, on the backs of insects,

streetlight by streetlight, endless blocks ahead

Clutch

Who wants this boxcar waiting,
these cardboard tubes?
I think everyone wants each other's
arms, those error-filled limbs
flailing everywhere but around us.

They pull you in just so
they can shove you away.
There's something to be said for that
whopping one person and it's not
chopped liver or potato salad or lemon

asparagus. Anthony, Tony, Antonio, it's all
comparable, the enemy, the friend,
the untrustworthy lover full
of charm's vandalism. If you try to escape,
they will betroth you

to a Dewey Dell unsweet and looking
for a fix. Simple to spectacular. No,
it's scrawling all over a beautiful postcard
and losing the return address. No, it's always been
the arms, inviting, full of loving harm.

The Miser(ables)

A fat(ter) girl boards the tour bus weari(ng) her "University Hot Stuff" tee and suddenly my shoes are miserable

The country Frenchman shoves his Mickey-hat(ted) daughter and suddenly I ha(te) him and mut(ter) something more miserable

Being the gut(ter) girl, the guttural listener is all *la la hmmm Napoleon la la mercy hmmm*

Yes, thrilled to be your spokeswo(man), America, no I'm being facetious, I'm still miserable, more so now than before

I say, dear sir, please step away from the window, France does not want to see your wiener

The Love Story

Here's the love
story minus the
story.

A
poor woman, in
poor health with
poor taste.

She shells the
vegetables into stereotypes in her long
vegetable garden.

Poverty was
funny and he has a wonderful sense
of humor.

Pancakes are
pancakes and his code for the
obscene which is a
shame because she still likes
breakfast.

The sky parades its
fucking
sunrise all the way to
sunset.

*A
sign of the
sighs,*
she ends.

Nothing Like Us

Paul Newman never looked like you
Rock Hudson didn't notice the ladies like you
But Richard Dawson kissed like you
And Desi Arnaz womanized like you

Like you, Spencer Tracy stayed with his wife
Kirk Douglas fucked like Spartacus
In the end we discover Laurence Olivier never loved Rebecca
Yul Brynner, the furrowed brow, majestic robes
Now I'm really pushing it, enter in column:

Nothing like you

I'm too fat to be Audrey Hepburn
Eyes too gray for Liz Taylor
I'm a little Vivien Leigh, a touch Joan Crawford
Scarlett and Dearest, brunette and mad
What I feel is red, like Lucille
Bongos over the Cuban
Cuban: unlike you

Yet exactly you

Quantity of the Quality

The heartbeat of the coupon-clipping classes
makes a government jittery

This time the pyramid of corpses
is not better them than me

And Roosevelt had syphilis, ya know, and
one out of four – those mealy mouths

Are the worst cases of all
the water is good, the cinema even better

And I love you
like the lover I won't

Trouble to kiss

Still Feeling It

still feeling fucked up and fake
still another day, still thick with hope

what a word wreck
what a display of linguistic insensitivity

a little something I call
rendered and insufficient

a little something I call
bohemian pain and one day

I'll be all right again
thankfully I can't keep making it new

there was a rare occurrence
I drank a bottle of wind

he looked at me strangely
I offered him

a Rolaid   this seemed
staged

this seemed
sentimental

Poem for Make-Believe

Your poems are not maps and

I'm lost

on a bus in France hauling bags

of cabbages

little cabbages, cute cabbages

cabbages with meaning

I'm not privy and I will

not eat and I will not boil

I will carry them home

plant them in my tendril garden

and ignore the urge to gag

Brunch with Cordelia

Wicked meals cost, so we're
not eating the bacon strips
not ordering coffee, not
buttering our toast.

Swine so sweet
we weep over
pancakes, those aren't our cruel
breasts steeping in syrup,

those ragged muffins are not
our morning kisses crusted and ignored.
Yesterday we were poolside, dancing
sugar canes, whisking mojitos.

This can't be our eulogy.
What about the quest for our
hearts and minds? Didn't anyone bother
sending a search party?

Requiem

Is it my turn to brush the tendrils from the table,
set service for two, apologize for elephants and kept pledges?

Does my grin and tingle still excite or are you somber now
like me? I'm small and strong, which is why I don't disrobe

even though I've been here smoothing and refolding napkins
for days, pining over our next funeral brunch. This is not the way I
       want it,

but I know the kind of creature you are and though I hate to admit
I too am part of this kindred tribe.

Off Vermont

Wasn't a leaf
that didn't
smack her face
on the way out
as she sped across
the green humps

There were road signs,
sharp turns, interstates,
omissions and a legacy
of mock repose
all clearly marked
so even girls could understand

This one kept her gaze
on the pretty man's chin, felt
sing-song wisps streaming
through her hair, down her spine,
bird songs or flashbacks –
is there such a translation?

Do lovers ever love? Of course
not, too obvious, better luck next time,
oh wait, there is no next time,
next in line, move along
Oh, don't worry, I'm going
Didn't stop

for syrup, wheels spat out
wry pine cones, provocation,

there it was, lie down and be
flattened, thank you, that *was* nice
crossing that turf was breech
without epidural
without child after ordeal
New York or Massachusetts,
the only options, she deserved nothing
more; two more locations to pretend,
for just a while, she's not tone deaf
small thoughts produce tiny tears and hers were
specks and plenty and would not wipe

Wifely Attempt at Poem

Only downright men deserve my slip

I'm trying to be a choice wife

My fidelity obscured by a poem gagging on the heyfull
panting on forced sophistication
A poem poemifying a woman and her persuasions until
it's absolutely ergo, egret

O hum, O sunk, O hasn't this heckled before?

My ankles stretch in a boneyard where
two skeletons are
familiar in that famished way

Only a man's chest never sheen is worthy of such errors

All fumble and March
All mind over grind
Maybe matted hair
I would not know

Began with the throat
Fell in love with a quotation I could not pronounce
He poemified a passage hoping I'd see myself
but the details were wanton, too pristine . . . no prissy
when reality was all flannel in flesh flambé
– a choice wife screaming "banshee!"

Yes, that's shameful

All this pretendography is driving me home
where I try to be a choice wife

Complications come from poemification
Suspected he was a vegetarian
with no middle name and no true age
Think he owes me an explanation
Think he owes me a sympathy letter
I think he should serve me tacos and offer
a tulip as sauvignon

His poems only poemified my thighs and didn't
mention I was trying to be a choice wife
while fists floundered, tongues clamped

There was a poetry reading held in a boneyard that
onlookers mistook for peep show
It should have been obvious
The aggrieved circled, fingered
my thoughtful frocks of fraught

for I was truly the choice wife

No Room at the Necropolis

When obstinance is a long wait and slight gift, we burn what we decorate and meet wearing funeral gowns and because we never go public, we never get our fill, always panting for the again and slipping through the already given. The card has five cups, three overturned, the lesson is simple and we understand and here we go trolling for graves in our mock white shrouds. *Ooooh, I'm a ghost and what a pretty tombstone! I want, I want, I want!* You lead, I follow, I lap. I'm lapping. Lapping the froth of this air that's supposed to be putrid, but I taste sweetmeat. You're digging. There's no soil. It's a hole and holes are empty and there you go, digging. There are instruments: violas and pianos sounding pure yet we fret over our off-key vocals and I try to loosen your collar and you accuse me of being a diva and I cry. You laugh, *Just joshing!* but I'm not laughing, I want to laugh, but so delicate and unwilling to make concessions and I want to concede, I want you to devour this victory, I want to lie down and accept my conquering all night long and I'm full of lies, a coffin of lies, and the more I want truth the more I lie because you will bury me with honesty, you will bury me with air thinking it's favor and so our errors pile, like bodies denied graves. This place does not want us, tells us to move on, find a coffee shop or motel, this is not the place of flesh and it is time to stop playing dead.

What There Wasn't Time to Mention

The ghost that woke and pinched soon became my uncle

The boy named Handmaker was a Jew Capricorn and a firefighter

They called with a code and brought eight years of atheism

He sang "I Got My Mind Set On You" and the dead deer no longer mattered

Fifteen

Favorite Monkee: Mickey

By the time I let him, I could barely stand him

My smile stopped a stick-up so they put me in an ark

It was Christmas and a fear of being punched and guilt of happiness and two months of bitter silence

Planes, Trains and Automobiles and M&M's

Once

Favorite Beatle: Paul

The one that got away was short and balding and I still can't believe it

Too much paint, ruined, nobody liked it, she threw it away

Threatened God, said *if you let this happen, I'll never pray again*

The boy from the trailer laced his shorts in front and rode his bike to my house

Her death should have been acknowledged

Our graffiti was foul and mean-spirited and written in crayon

Favorite Menudo member: Roy

It cost $9.99 and felt sleazy and invasive but I wasn't about to ask and she said she needed to know

He was asleep when I found it

Lied and said my name was "Sammy Jo" because she was the prettiest on *Dynasty*

Well, it's eight now

It was called "Look at the Sky" and the refrain: "Isn't it pretty?"

Embarrassing childhood crush: David Letterman

An invitation should be acknowledged

It was never about love, it was about falling behind and being the last one

The other became a police officer and made sergeant and headlines

A basement floor, under a blanket

Seemed bigger the first time around

That time the promise was kept

It's true, watched it happen and thought *peace the fuck out, indeed*

One time I painted my face so pale they said *don't do that again, be sweet for children*

She accused me of knowing, the physical description, state of residence and initial, accurate

Less embarrassing childhood crush: Lou Diamond Phillips

Twenty years later: maybe she made up that ten-foot pole comment

Stole from the register and put gas in my Buick

The bad man was a prison guard and I wasn't who he wanted, but was the one alone and drunk and asleep on a sofa

Little memory exists of atheism, but occasionally old scriptures surface

Pretty spelled *pity*

Nothing fake about keeping up appearances

The rest were soldiers, I was the priest, healer or medic, depending on the century

By the time the New Kids were on the Block, there was no need,
I had breasts

By telling these things, it will be everything and it will be finished

Mozzarella, squash, popcorn

Rare Hawk Evident

Hawk yes, freeway lifted flock
thick in soup, all apology
following white wiseacres.
Hawk maybe not.
Hawk faint on air.
Hawk die on beige.
Cougars run the turnip fields,
eating seed catalogues,
banking in pants,
barking barnstormers,
what we call authorized curiosities.
She keeps a journal of Hawaiians,
there were notable leis.
Wet rub, dry rub,
the last of the yellow cake
happy blondness
breathless beige.
Hawk not so notch.
She found her pygmy gabba aphrodisiac
because she *is* alone.

Burgers and Pitchforks

The Man with the Pretty Chin [laughing]: Does my leaving before dawn make you feel cheap?

The Smitten Girl: You are nameless and you are despair and you are what I want. You will not wound, maim, kill or otherwise hurt. You are unpleasant and you are survivable. Somewhere I know what you are – and remember when I see, hear, touch and taste and am always surprised. Your job is to numb and sometimes you make me your little zombie. And sometimes, I bite your neck.

The Heart Specter: You a(re des)pair that's lost its (s)mitten.

The Spirit to Adopt

She thought she was going to die, he never returned
her messages, but eventually he did and by then
she remembered he was a cowardly moral relativist
and all she wanted was witty banter fucking.

On Realizing There Won't Be a Ceremony

Don't call me feminine and excessive and screw you, I know that temple, I took her picture and it's she who doesn't remember me, the only one who knew to bring a red fritter to the reception. She thinks she's cute and I'm impressed with her sanctity and her little pews too.

Finite and Fortnight

Boys are so cruel

coal-crushing Martians, rope-humping punks

store these jars, a bare season cometh, don't mind the boys

they're maintaining the order, poking holes in bicycle wheels

innovating their penises, splendid little stabbing machines

this is where they bypass our love, fuck from windows

never return our binoculars

it's time to flush the medication

it's time to wise up

the boys whisper *this is what I miss most*

it's an honor, it's 15 minutes, we're dismal

pigeonholed, shoveling coal

Ours Alone

our udders bare, our udders bad, our misunderstanding
who's the cow and who's for free?

I got your invisible thread, I got it right through here
bah!, that's one fucked frequency you got

and I got your throwaway phrase
kissing, wow, makes me feel downtown

that little possibility lovers stopped negotiating
here's where the barnyard ends

so tired, scratching words, sad sad devils
all I wanted, surprise, surmise, circumcised

Kinda, Yeah

Call it a flash flaw

more than 50 words needed

nothing like abstinence to help saturate that page, eh?

I kinda hate you

However you chose to paw that mole

I kinda need more time

to make these verbs gasp

swirl that blatant innuendo deep

into your collar's swallow

Who the Man Was

…and he was the spike in my dream
scar circling my wrist
he was mother's whimper
father's brown shoe lace
shredded and trampled
found his way into everything
inhabited my pupils
gnawed ear drums, swung nostril to
nostril, rested on upper lip fuzz
he rented on Ellsworth, owned on
Summerlea, murdered on Elmer
all charm and vomit
burgers and pitch forks
I filed a restraining order
asked for his hand in marriage

Luna Park (1907 – 1916)

When nothing better bubbled your kiln
you looked for entrance.
Why not? It was safe for you,

the lions only ate women.
You saw castle and carousel
never shades and shadows.   She

fastened her belt, endured the scenic
railway until everything throbbed
riot, licked cotton candy while you

twirled the cardboard cone. You said
Shoot the Chute, she said
Temple of Mystery, you

jumped the turnstile
yelling after the trolley.
Desires vanish once you

leave, it's always different on return.
Rainchecks bring ash, perhaps a fond
brief flash, moonstruck girl

breast stroke, mighty Monongahela.

Wanting to Be a Man of Saturn

On Saturn men stretch through lovers like cotton candy, sticky white cones decompose seamlessly into the soil after a few rotations. (Light scrubbing removes the pink taste from any face.)

It's a bountiful planet with no greed or violence or laws because the men of Saturn smartly swallow their children. (I tried to keep mine inside; they kicked and punched and were too much.)

The men of Saturn are Titans. They breed sickles and yard work. (I tried out for the Titans, but couldn't do a cartwheel. Or a split. Too uptight to flip. I feared grass stains and strained hips.)

The men of Saturn aren't novas and aren't my friends. They're mighty with envious rings and hidden offspring. They finger the nymphs who suckle them. Sugary and brutal and quick to retract. They neither profess nor propose for shackles don't clamp candor. (They tell you their name is *Sani* when their driver's licenses read *Zuhal*.)

My Lover Never

Matrimony had a lover;
they took bike rides together,

shared an angel sex partner,
tied her to a cement block and utterly rejected her.

My lover never gave a handjob
in the muck, hardly.

My lover is a sex lamb, incensed
and salmon-colored

like that man over there,
pruning his foreign foliage, ignoring me.

Awfully American, pretending not.
A fancy American wearing stripes.

I'm wearing a skirt.
I tried to call, a little hurt.

Attending yet another wedding.
My lover pumps a bright bicycle,

hoards wire hangers, licks moths,
finds pleasures inside his mouth.

Love, we must atone some.
Something inside must climb and crinkle.

You were never supposed to be my friend.
That's passion's funny lie.

Retention

The sleigh is full of suitcases

Suitcases full of mammaries

These mammaries weigh me down

The sleigh is a wooden toboggan
that's never been waxed

I never saw a sleigh trip
over a snowflake before
nor been quite so charmed by
a song about child abuse

Lugging around this extra weight
makes glaciers seem speedy
– that one over there,
I've named it "Lucas's Ejaculation"

An only recollection of a one-time sweetheart

Brevity Is Not my Soul

for a few minutes, I tricked myself

placed faith in the talent of fingers

speculated past lives wanted relived

it ended and it never began

blurry as truth, I

averted more than eyes

no future tryst scheduled, our ankles

never to entwine again, and this was your

aspiration, you always understood and it

occurred and it didn't occur to you

just how unjaded I was clasping hands

here I am, conjuring more liability

here I am, spare one moment more, spy my

tripping, a paper trail of failed chants and exhibits

a few scratched lines I pray will suffice

Apologies for Ice

No bread crumbs or constellations
I see nothing
except thick trunks, leafy branches
Now is not the time for snow
but I pray for it anyway
it's crisp and puts me sleep
Charm brings distrust
wolves, June fools
It's almost July
Grandma passed away, the wolf
missed his chance and
doesn't know what to do with himself
I squandered mine
fill freezer trays with water
stockpile limes just in case
you stop by for a vodka tonic
You're busy demonstrating your
quaint breeding for elegant cruelty
ignore, then apologize beautifully
seize upon the cold retort
now I'm the asshole swinging the
hatchet with no regard for school children
So I bide my time sipping seltzer with the
animal meant to gobble Grandma
People judge, disapprove
yet he was the only one to
send condolences, start a dialogue
I'm lonesome with no one else
My winter valley upbringing
taught me all skiers end up

dead, twisted in the gully
their locust eyes frozen like feelings
still able to gaze upon our abundant shortcomings
as we pile their corpses on the wagon
which is why my people
keep their love on a switch
flip it off and tape it down
Too bad about electricity
once I was thankful for it
I will be again in
another life, said sadly, fondly

Cold Storage

farewell to frosty things   to that shivering shoebox

if sentiment means making cabbage of things

if cabbage presumes intimacy

if silence weaves tongues

if the city signals tendrils

if tendrils are wintered and false

the ankle cramp   the shrivel   all bloody mary mix

all hoarse   all ice   all daggers and sugar cubes

darling, it's time

if all you can come up with is a thought

adieu

Much We Could Do

What's even worse
are those folks who ignore and
abuse us while pretending to
dote on and adore us
make us their pasty white gravy
never taking a biscuit.
Oh, they'll show us their lipsticks
remind us how their hands
separate the person from the body
slip the trinkets out our pockets.
There's much we could do
if we wanted to forget.
We could ride buses and collect transfers.
We could make charts, predict our next
bland predicaments, our laments.
We could smell like beer and
never leave the upstairs.

Whatnot Tribute
a collaboration with Anthony Robinson

Should have kissed your kneecap instead of calling
My nurse, my pretty little bump, my special hump in the front

On the porch swing with my triple beam, weighing up grams,
Should have kissed your pretty place, all pinked

And succotashed, all flush and livermashed, all knowing
And albeit nevermine, nevermine, nevermind

Don't undermine my serial slump, my frequent melancholic
Piece of vitriol, my affection for your birthmarked heart

It's a ruse, a rooskie in a flea market peddling pins that I
Sink into a pretty cloth doll, she resembles you, all hushed

And trammeled, trampling your foes with a straight flush,
Chasing the poker boys back to the blow-hole

The sink-hole, the deep bowl, the spin till spun
Spun till span, it's your hand grazing, steam hazing

And the final lazy bastards who stole all your Purina – If
It's difficult to forgive it's probably worth crossing over.

Sestina! That's what I forgot to write for you, see I'm
Blushing. I'm sorry, so sorry, so sodden and Gomorrah.

Acknowledgements

Some of the poems in this book have appeared in the following publications: *MiPOesias, Coconut, Kulture Vulture, Tool a Magazine, The Carolina Quarterly, mem, SOFTBLOW, Melancholia's Tremulous Dreadlocks, The Hat, past simple, The Concher, Jumps, OCHO, The Bedside Guide to No Tell Motel, The Bedside Guide to No Tell Motel – Second Floor, The Displayer, The Fishouse, Beltway Poetry Quarterly* and *Vs.*

My indebtedness to dear friend and editor, Bruce Covey, for his support and generosity.

Thank you to the following people who have assisted with and/or inspired (whether knowingly or unknowingly) poems in this book: Jill Alexander Essbaum, Anthony Robinson, David Lehman, PF Potvin, Charles Jensen, Rebecca Loudon, Meghan Punschke, Joseph Massey, Lorna Dee Cervantes, Brent Terry, Aaron Belz, Cyndi Lauper and former President Bill Clinton.

"Clutch," "My Lover Never," "Still Feeling It" and "Much We Could Do" are dedicated to my blog buddy, Anthony Robinson.

Love and all earthly gratitude to my two favorite guys – Chris Morrow and Gideon Hart Morrow.

About the Author

Born and raised in Pittsburgh, Pennsylvania, Reb Livingston (www.reblivingston.net) now lives in Northern Virginia with her husband and son. She's the editor of *No Tell Motel* (www.notellmotel.org) and publisher of No Tell Books (www.notellbooks.org). Her poem "That's Not Butter" is anthologized in *Best American Poetry 2006* (Scribner).

www.ingramcontent.com/pod-product-compliance
Ingram Content Group UK Ltd.
Pitfield, Milton Keynes, MK11 3LW, UK
UKHW041434180426